T0146698

Klassy

Written and Published
By Kristin Lee Carro
From 1972 to 2014

authorHOUSE®

AuthorHouse™
1663 Liberty Drive
Bloomington, IN 47403
www.authorhouse.com
Phone: 1 (800) 839-8640

Published by AuthorHouse   04/10/2017

ISBN: 978-1-5246-8747-2 (sc)
ISBN: 978-1-5246-8746-5 (e)

My name is Kristin Lee Carro. I was born as Kristin Lee Nowatske in Milwaukee, Wisconsin on February 23, 1972. My first memories were visits to my grandparents. I was glad to have the most encouraging, loving, caring, Grandma that most people would love to have. To begin with, she was the one that encouraged me to follow my dreams no matter what it took. She also said to me to just do my best at my accomplishments, and my dreams, and they would come true. She also told me if I do my best I will be successful at whatever I choose to do in life. My grandma was an amazing baker. I remember when I came in from playing outside she would have hot apple pie waiting for me on the table. I would walk in the house and the

apple pie had an aroma that took my breath away. My grandma had a long lace, bordered white table cloth on a square wood table. The four chairs that were around the table were hard as a rock. Due to my grandma's old age and inability to reach on the left side of the table, she had a stack of baking sheets and bowls to make it easier for her to access. Like my grandma, her apartment building was old and frail. Walking up the stairs, the door was hard to open. Upon entering her two bed room apartment there was a loveseat couch on the left hand side and there was a plaid recliner chair on the right hand side. The carpet was faded brown and it didn't have much padding or thickness to it. Her apartment was always cold and damp. The furnace was old and made a ruckus noise. My grandma stood 5'2" tall and she had short gray hair. Her voice was soft spoken and she spoke words of wisdom. She would tell me that school would be hard. I often remember her words when

I was in English classes and I'd get frustrated with essays writing. I'd tell myself, I can't do this. I would than think about what she told me and it would give me the strength to move forward and just do it. My grandma would also tell me that not everyone that enters my life will be nice. She'd say not to pay attention to them and move forward. When I was in high school I was teased for being in special education classes. I remember one girl calling me stupid and dumb. It hurt my feelings and I wanted to hit her but, I didn't because, I didn't want to get in trouble. I remembered what my grandma had told me. As I previously mentioned my grandma was an amazing baker and taught me how to bake. I remember when she tried to teach me how to make apple pie. It was a complete disaster. As I rolled out the dough, it just fell apart and the flour was all over the floor and my face. Then she told me to sprinkle nut Meg in and I had that all over the floor and counter. After

that disaster, she was laughing and had told me if I want apple pie just buy it at the store. She then decided to teach me how to make brownies. They turned out very well, she told me to stick with making brownies. We both had a taste when the first batch came out of the oven. She said these are yummy and moist! I still make them it reminds me of when I had make them with her Up until I was six years old we lived in Wisconsin. We would visit my grandma in Wisconsin every week. Once we moved to California the visits were once to twice a year. But, we stayed in contact by phone. We would call her about once a month and she would ask me how school was going. As I grew older the conversations with her have stuck with me. Her advice and words of wisdom have helped me through life. Overall, I had fond memories of Wisconsin and family gatherings there. For instance, when I was little my parents owned a motel and restaurant and when my sister would

babysit me she would give me packages of bread sticks individually wrapped every time I would cry, they were really good. The chef that worked there made us anything we wanted to eat. Every summer my family and I would always go to a large music festival called summer fest. It was held at Henry Maier Park in Milwaukee, Wisconsin where there would be live bands and lots of food. We always had a lot of fun when we went. I also have fond memories growing up. In the back of the elementary school adjacent to the park. The pond would freeze where my sister and I would go ice skating. There was a warm house near the pond where we went to put our skates on. Before my sister and I went skating, I remember getting mad at her because she would put on my mittens and I didn't want them on. After skating we went to the candy store that was down the street from the house. The winters were cold in Wisconsin but, they stand in memory because of the special

activities my family and I did during the season. Why my grandma is important to me. I would like to share the grandma that comes to mind her name is Ruth Rogers. She loved me unconditionally and special. My grandma is a very special person to me because she taught and showed me how to bake. She was always there for me. She was kind, caring, loving grandma that other grandchildren would love to have. She was always so eager to ask me how I was doing in school every time I would talk with her on the phone. She would always give me some encouragement throughout my life. After my surgery, my parents received a phone call from my aunt in Wisconsin that my grandma was in the hospital. We flew out the next day. A few days later she passed away. I was heartbroken because, she was my favorite grandma but, her spirit is with me. As I remember, I would go to Wisconsin a few times to visit my aunt, uncle and cousins and also go see my birth father and other grandma. I would

stay with my dad for a couple days and my other grandma a couple of days. My other grandma and I used to go to fancy dinners and just had fun visiting. I stayed at my other grandma. She would take me to get my nails done. After my nail appointment, my other grandma and dad would take me to a fancy dinner. We would always go to his favorite breakfast place called George webs. Before I left my dad's, he would take me clothes shopping so, then it was time to say goodbye to fly back to California Shorty after, I left my birth father passed away in 2001.

In 1978, my mom, sister and I moved California from Wisconsin where I was at that time. We stayed with my aunt and uncle and my two cousins in Carlsbad until we found a place to live. One summer day I went outside to ride my big wheel down the street but, before I got down the street I only got as far as next door, I ran over the next door neighbors sprinkle head. The man who lived

there came out and said hi than, he went next door as I rode down the street. The man from next door went to meet my mom. They liked each other, and decided to date. After a month, or so, we had moved out of my aunt and uncles house. We moved to Mira Mesa. I don't remember too much because I was only 7 years old. I enjoyed when my grandparents would visit. One day my mom went to work and my grandma cut my hair. When my mom came home from work. She got mad at my grandma for cutting my hair. It was time for my grandparents to fly back to Wisconsin, so, at that point My mom had to hire a babysitter while she went to work. The woman she hired was an awful babysitter. In 1979, we moved from Mira Mesa to Penaquitas. We lived in a two bedroom apartment. My mom got married. My grandparents came out to babysit me while my parents went on their honeymoon. I enjoyed visits with my grandparents. When my parents came back that is when they had

to fly back to Wisconsin. I enjoyed living in Penaquitas because; the school I went to was up the street from where I lived. I also met some friends there. We moved from Penaquitas to Pt. Mugu where my dad got stationed there. We lived in a two bedroom house on a navy base. My sister Kari gave me a great gift which is my baby nephew. In 1980, we left Pt. Mugu. I enjoyed living in Pt. Mugu because; of the navy base, we always used to go to the officers club for dinners and dancing. The bartender painted a picture of a little girl and called it little Kristin. We moved to Camarillo because; my dad got stationed to go out there. When we first got to Camarillo my parents enrolled me in Camarillo Elementary school right away. When I first started there it took me awhile to adjust. I met some nice student's there. I also met a really nice teacher. There was this one girl that showed me around the school. We became friends her name is Terri Grob. We always looked forward

spending time together and as time went on we became best friends. We were inseparable. I also remember the class took field trip to my teacher's house where everybody made homemade ice cream. I also remember going to a fall carnival where my parents worked the popcorn booth. I had lots of fun and memories living in Camarillo. I didn't always like to move around a lot but, when the navy gives you orders to move you need to take them. We went from Camarillo to Fair fax, Virginia we had stayed there for a couple of years. I enjoyed living in Fair fax, Virginia because; we lived in a two story house. I really enjoyed it when it snowed and when my sister's boyfriend came over. One night he came over to pick up my sister and I opened the door couldn't believe my eyes. We moved from Fair fax, Virginia back to the original house in Carlsbad. Not long after moving back to Carlsbad I remember my parents and I flew into New Jersey my aunt and uncle picked us

up from the airport. We stayed at my grandparents' house for one week. The next day we went on a ferry boat around New York City. We saw parts of Manhattan as well as the statue of liberty. My aunt, uncle, cousins and my parents and I drove from New York City to Philadelphia to see the broad way play called Annie. When we left Philadelphia we could go visit my other grandparents in Moorestown, New Jersey. We stayed at their house I always remembered having fun and having crab parties. My grandma would make her homemade Manahan clam chowder and my grandpa would get the crabs ready for us to eat. My grandpa would also marinade the meat for hoagie sandwiches. He would make them yummy! My aunt, uncle and cousins came over to visit. We all had a feast after, we had are feast all of us went down to the basement to play pool. We drove from Moorestown, New Jersey to New York City. As I remember, visiting my grandparents, aunt, uncle and cousins

we would go to Atlantic City where they would vacation there every year. One day we went with them and I was making a sandcastle with my cousins. I decided to go in the ocean to swim and big wave came towards me and sweep me under. I didn't know what had happened after, I came up the big wave was so strong it had snapped my bathing suit top off. I was very scared that was the last time I went in the ocean. We could not visit all the time so, our visits were once a year but, we stayed in contact by phone all the time. We came back to Carlsbad. Before my sister had moved to La. Habra she was living in a one bedroom apartment with her son Christopher in San Marcos. One day my sister Kari met a really nice man who she dated for a long time. Then the three moved in together now Kari and Ed lives in a two bedroom home in La Habra. As far as my nephew, he turned out to be a handsome young man. He moved to Texas for one year in his early 20's and I was very

sad. I don't know what sparked that idea, but he decided to come back and that is when he met Tiffany. He is now married to a nice young lady. He and Tiffany have three kids; Jordan, Chris, and Ethan. They also live in La Habra in a three bedroom house. I was in high school at the time when my mom asked me if I want a dog. I said yes. I had my first dog, her name was Sheba. My mom and I drove down to point Loma where the lady lived to see the dog. Sheba was a rescue dog. When I saw her she came running up to me and lick my face and after I saw her I wanted to take her home. She was a princess. When we gave her treats she would take them like a lady. Before walking her she would sit by the door waiting for me to put on her leach. A month after I got her, my parents enrolled me in San Marcos High school as I remember; I enjoyed San Marcos junior High school. I had really nice teachers, good friends and great classes. When I went into San Marcos high

school, I didn't do so well. I had gone down the wrong path which was hanging out with the wrong people, being teased, and getting into trouble a lot. For example, I would be teased for being in special classes. I remember I wanted to hang around this one group but, they told me to go away. I would get in trouble a lot because; I would ditch classes and go across the street to Carl's Jr. and miss 5th period. I was trying to fit in with the other students but, it just got me in trouble all the time. When I was in high school, I remember taking a night class at the Vista adult school to get my ROP certificate for child development. I had taken a summer job at a preschool that entitled me to get the certificate. One day the principal called my parents about my bad behavior. I made better grades and had shaped up and did better in school. After the phone call, I was grounded for one week. That is when my parents taught me the importance to have good values thru life. I'm lucky to have the

loving, caring, support of family. They give me encouragement and strong family values. I have learned from my family the importance of education how gaining my independence will help me in life and the importance of living my life with integrity. I choose these values because they are the values that have helped me get to where I am today. Family values give me a strong foundation for life! To begin with, my parents taught me to do well in school and get good grades. My dad studied with me. He taught me to always spend time to study. To achieve my goals I learned to make time to study because if I don't I would lose out on life chances. He encouraged me to work hard at my studies. I am a persistent person. I learned the importance of getting a good education from my parents. I remember when I was living with my parents Barneys owner died and her sister took Barney to the vet to put him to sleep. My cousin had worked there she told the lady no. She

took Barney to my aunt's and uncle's house. I lived with my parents at the time. My aunt, uncle lived next door that is how I saw Barney all the time. I used to always babysit Barney. They went on road trips. One day I was next door and Barney was out front on his leash. He got out of his leash and was at my parent's front door. He kept running away to my parents' house so, that is when my aunt, uncle gave me Barney. I met this one guy at Palomar College and we dated for a while than we decided to move in together, it was great for a while but, than it went very sour because, I went to jail. One day my boyfriend went to work, I made lunch for the couple that was staying with us the girl called the cops when they came she told the cops that I was steeling and had drugs so, they took in me and I stayed overnight, but they could not keep me in jail because, I did not do anything. I went to jail for someone else's mistake, the cops were after my boyfriend. They could not get him

so, they got me instead. the cops were after my boyfriend. They could not get him so, they got me instead. That night I moved back in with my parents. A while later, I met this one girl and we hung out almost every day. One day she came over and had her dog with her. During Christmas time she bought her dog Cricket over to visit. One day after Christmas. She decided to give me Cricket. My parents and I gave her a happy life. Shortly after meeting her, I took several classes up until I got in my apartment. I lived with my boyfriend in Vista before this. Things went sour between us, he moved out and I stayed until the lease was up. One day my mom called and told me my aunt Jill was in the hospital. The next day my mom picked me up and took me to the hospital so, I can see her but, I can only pray she knew I was there because, she was in a coma shortly after, and she passed away. I do miss my aunt so much. My mom, aunt, and I used to always go shopping together and after we

would go to lunch. My aunt would always have dinner parties at her condo in San Marcos, family gathering and Christmas parties. We all had a lot of fun together.

Four years ago, I went through a section eight program with the help of my parents. It is a low income program. Now I am living in a one bedroom apartment by the beach. I almost got kicked off section eight because, I met a guy and we were hanging out every day; so I had asked him if he would like to stay with me. One day my manager came to my door with a notice to move out, but he moved out and I stayed. My manager is a wonderful person to let me stay in my apartment. Since I'm living on my own has helped me have self-confidence. I went back to Mira Costa College and took some Basic English courses then finish with my basics then when I enrolled in English 100. I had got sick so I had to withdraw from class. This went on for three

months finally, I went to get a referral to have a scope down my throat and it was scheduled for December 2 for an endoscopy and my doctor found extreme inflammation I take 2 different medications for my acid reflex problem. I need to watch my diet for certain foods and beverages to avoid. It is an ongoing condition. Finally, after four months I'm back at the City of Carlsbad Library. I did my assessment on April 29, 2014 and the staff found me a tutor on June 11, 2014. I'm learning to solve my own life issues and problems. I'm glad my parents taught me the values of independence because I am now very responsible women who can life on my own. Three years ago, my mom had got ill and was in the hospital for a while. I don't know what sparked the idea but, my dad and I went to the Camp Pendleton animal shelter to find a dog. We arrived at the animal shelter. We walked up to the gate and my dad asked if there was any medium size dog. The lady went inside

the kennel to look. My dad and I stayed outside to wait for a dog to come out. A little tan dog came running up to greet us and that is how I got Rocky. As we were leaving the shelter I looked at my dad and asked what is mom going to say? My Dad and I used to visit my mom in the hospital and we took Rocky on road trips every time. We would go down there. Rocky is a funny dog because when I give him a treat he hides it in the leather couch or around the corner. He is a cutie pie because when I come over to visit he greets me at the door with his stuffed animal in his month. He is also feisty when my dad takes him for a walk and he gets the leash and puts it in his month like he is chewing on the leash. He also gets feisty when my mom gives him treats too. He gives us a lot of affection. Overall, he is a very good dog and we love him. March of 2013, the scariest thing I have gone through is getting a biopsy and surgery because a lump was found during a routine mammogram.

I had to wait a month before my surgery was scheduled. It was very stressful because I had too much time to worry finally, the nurse called to say my biopsy was scheduled for March 29. I entered Scripps hospital in La Jolla. I had to go to the breast cancer center to get a needle biopsy. This was done before I had my surgery to remove a tumor. The nurse wheeled me in the operation room and they gave me a shot to go to sleep. When the procedure was done the nurse wheeled me in the recovery room. My mom and dad were loving, and supportive throughout my surgery. That same day, I went to my parent's house. My parents took care of me until I recovered my dog rocky was by my side the whole time cuddling with me while I sleep if I hadn't had the surgery the tumor could have developed into breast cancer. I couldn't take the chance. I guess you could say was giving a second chance it was a scary thing because I didn't understand why this was happening to me. Thank

you God! With this second chance I am eating healthier, walking more and researching recipes for a better healthier life. I have faced challenges, including special education classes, being teased and bullied in school, and spending many years living with my parents before becoming an independent adult, it is important to me to write my story. Perhaps by writing this I can help others with their challenges and help them realize they can reach their goals. To improve my writing skills I have taken several English classes at Mira Costa College. I am making good progress in my writing skills. Now I know the steps to take to become a better writing. First, before you write a story it is helpful to a prewritten, outline, brainstorming and a cluster map to bring your ideas together. You also need to have the proper punctuation. It is also important to have good sentence structure. You need to have good clear sentences to help you stay on track and emphasize the subject your writing

about. My story would inspire several people with their challenges and they would benefit from my story I would like to be able to tell people that it is not impossible to reach their goals with difficult challenges by facing many challenges and becoming independent now, I'm a strong and resilient adult.   Five years ago, most people told me I could not to go back to college, which is when I met my counselor. She encouraged me to go back to college, I am glad I did because; I accomplished all good things in life.

The End

I would like to thank and recognize the following people for all their support while writing my autobiography. Janet Carro, Stephen Carro, Kari Nowatske, Ed Holmes

Thanks again